FAR-OUT and UNUSUAL

RATS

pets

Cool Pets!

Enslow Elementary
an imprint of

Enslow Publishers, Inc.
40 Industrial Road
Box 398
Berkeley Heights, NJ 07922
USA

http://www.enslow.com

Alvin and Virginia Silverstein
and Laura Silverstein Nunn

Enslow Elementary, an imprint of Enslow Publishers, Inc.

Enslow Elementary® is a registered trademark of Enslow Publishers, Inc.

Library of Congress Cataloging-in-Publication Data
Silverstein, Alvin.
    Rats : cool pets! / Alvin Silverstein, Virginia Silverstein and Laura Silverstein Nunn.
        p. cm. — (Far-out and unusual pets series)
    Includes index.
    Summary: "Provides basic information about rats and keeping them as pets"—Provided by publisher.
    ISBN 978-0-7660-3882-0
    1. Rats as pets—Juvenile literature. I. Silverstein, Virginia B. II. Nunn, Laura Silverstein. III. Title.
    SF459.R3S55 2011
    636.935'2—dc22
                                2010054004
Future editions:
Paperback ISBN 978-1-4644-0127-5
ePub ISBN 978-1-4645-1034-2
PDF ISBN 978-1-4646-1034-9

Printed in the United States of America
012012 The HF Group, North Manchester, IN
10 9 8 7 6 5 4 3 2 1

To Our Readers: We have done our best to make sure all Internet Addresses in this book were active and appropriate when we went to press. However, the author and the publisher have no control over and assume no liability for the material available on those Internet sites or on other Web sites they may link to. Any comments or suggestions can be sent by e-mail to comments@enslow.com or to the address on the back cover.

Photo Credits: An Aqouti Rex Rat that won Best Rex at an AFRMA show. Photo by Craig Robbins, p. 14 (bottom left); Associated Press, p. 26; Best Pet Rat—This young girl's Burmese rat won Best Pet Rat Youth at an AFRMA show. Photo by Karen Robbins, p. 43; Carol Lawton, Blue Shuze Rodentry, pp. 32, 34; Hattie McRattie, p. 3; © Imagestate Media Partners Limited - Impact Photos/Alamy, p. 6; Photo Researchers, Inc.: Nigel Cattlin, p. 28, Will & Deni McIntyre, p. 41; Photo taken by Cathleen S. Schneider Russell (2008) (top left); Photo by Geri Hauser, p. 16; Photo by Larry Ferris, p. 39; Photo by Nichole Royer, p. 14 (bottom right); Shutterstock.com, pp. 4, 7, 8, 11, 12, 14 (top right), 15, 17, 18, 20, 22–23, 25, 30, 36, 44; © Steve Welsh/Alamy, p. 21.

Illustration Credits: © 2011 Gerald Kelley, www.geraldkelley.com

Cover Photo: Shutterstock.com

Contents

Rats can be smart and loving pets.

1

Oh, Rats!

Eek! Just the thought of rats scurrying around makes most people want to run and hide. Everybody *knows* that rats are dirty, disease-carrying animals, right? Wrong! This may be true of wild rats from the city sewer. But not all rats deserve this bad reputation. In fact, some rats can actually make great pets. These pet rats are very different from wild rats. Tame rats are friendly, smart, and lovable animals.

Rats look like giant mice. In fact, some people think mice grow up to be rats. That's not true. They belong to the same animal family, but there are some differences between them. The most

Going Wild

Imagine thousands of wild rats coming together in one place. Sound like a nightmare? It might be to some people, but not in India. Rats are actually treated like gods in India. It's true! There is a temple in a small town in India where people come to worship the rats that live there. The temple is home to around 20,000 rats! The Indian people bring food for the rats. They talk to them. They touch them. They even think it's lucky when the rats scurry over their bare feet!

noticeable one is their size. A rat is about three to four times as big as a mouse. It is also about ten times heavier!

What you might not know is that rats are much smarter than mice. In fact, some people say that rats are just as smart as dogs. They can learn to do tricks. They also love to cuddle with their owners.

Pet rats are not simply *tamed* wild rats. You can't just pick up a rat from the street and expect it to become a sweet, lovable pet. It doesn't work that way. Many years ago, people decided to breed (raise) rats. The rats they chose were

The top picture is a rat, and the bottom is a mouse. Can you tell the difference?

With proper care, rats can be great pets for kids.

wild, but the breeders picked only the friendliest, most gentle rats to have babies together. Years of breeding changed these rats. They lost their "wildness." They were not nervous. They did not run away or attack when a person approached them. (That's what wild rats would do.) Today's tame rats are calm, friendly, and curious creatures.

Rats can make great pets for kids. They are a lot of fun and love to play games. But keeping pet rats is a big responsibility. Learn everything you can before you make your decision. With the right care, most rats live for two to three years— although some may live up to six.

Read on and find out what makes rats such far-out and unusual pets.

2

Choosing Your Very Own Rats

Why would someone choose a rat for a pet? Why not a gerbil, a hamster, or a mouse? Unlike most small pets, pet rats rarely bite people. In fact, they are more likely to lick you. Tame rats love to be handled and be a part of the family. So the question is, "Why *not* a pet rat?"

Rats Up Close

Have you ever heard people say they have seen a rat "as big as a cat?" Actually, that is not possible. Rats may be big, but they're not *that* big.

Far
Out!

The First Pet Rats

Keeping rats as pets is not a recent thing. It started well over a hundred years ago. At that time, rat killing was a popular sport. In London, people placed bets on whose dog could kill the most rats in the shortest time. Hundreds of wild rats were trapped and used for this sport. Sometimes unusual-looking rats were caught, including white ones with pink eyes. Some of these white rats were kept and bred. These rats most likely were the first pet rats.

They usually weigh about one pound (450 grams). Some males may weigh as much as two pounds (more than 900 grams). Adult rats are about eight to ten inches (20 to 25 cm) long from the tip of the nose to the start of the tail.

Rats also have a long tail, about eight to ten inches (20 to 25 cm) long. That's as long as a rat's body. The tail is not covered with fur like the rest of the body. Some people are grossed out by the rat's long, naked tail. They think it looks like a worm or a slithering snake. Actually, the tail is not totally bare. It is covered with tiny bristly hairs.

Rat tails have tiny bristly hairs.

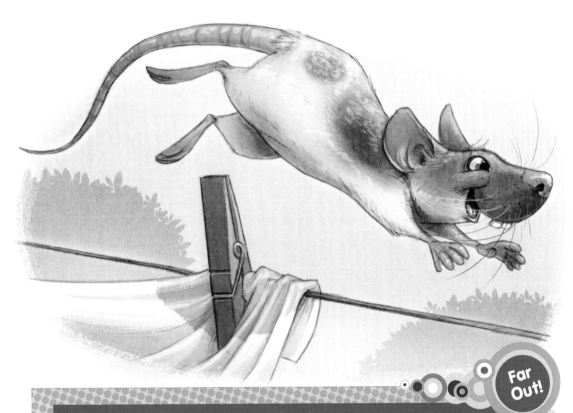

Rat Tails

A rat's tail might not be pretty to some people, but it's very important to the animal. For one thing, the long tail helps the rat keep its balance. When the rat runs, for example, it doesn't drag its tail behind it. It keeps the tail slightly above the ground. If the rat moves along a narrow surface, such as a rope, it will swing its tail from side to side. (Tightrope walkers do something like that, too. They move a pole from side to side to help keep their balance.) When the rat is on a moving object, such as its owner's shoulder, it will curl its tail under or around the object to keep its balance.

Hooded rat

Pet rats come in many different colors. White rats usually have pink eyes. Other fur colors may include black, dark brown ("chocolate"), tan, gray, blue, lilac, and a number of other shades. The fur may be a solid color or it may have various markings. Hooded rats are a common type. These rats have white bodies with a dark-colored head and a stripe running down the back. A rat's fur is usually straight and smooth. But some rats have curly fur and even curly whiskers.

Siamese rat

Curly rat

Fawn rat

Unusual Rats

Some kinds of pet rats are *really* unusual. One type is called a dumbo. A dumbo rat has larger, wider ears than a typical rat. The ears are also lower on the head. (These rats are named for the cartoon character, Dumbo the elephant.)

Dumbo rats have larger ears than other rats.

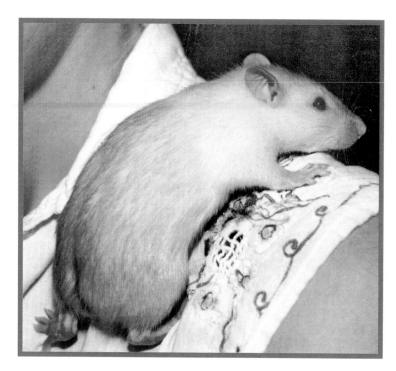

One type of rat is a tailless rat. They are born without tails.

Another uncommon kind is the tailless rat. It is born with no tail at all. Tailless rats are usually smaller than normal rats. Many tailless rats hop instead of walk.

The hairless rat is another unusual type. This rat is completely naked—it has no fur on its body or tail. Needless to say, hairless rats can get chilled very easily. (These rats should probably wear a rat-sized sweater to keep warm. Yes, pet stores do sell them!)

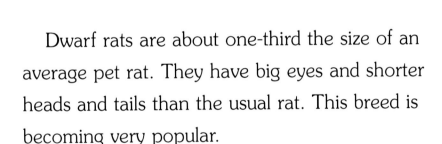

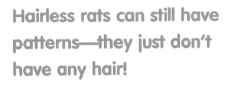
Hairless rats can still have patterns—they just don't have any hair!

Dwarf rats are about one-third the size of an average pet rat. They have big eyes and shorter heads and tails than the usual rat. This breed is becoming very popular.

Where Do You Buy Pet Rats?

Probably the best place to get pet rats is from a responsible rat breeder. These breeders take special care of their animals. They keep an eye on the rats to make sure they stay healthy. They also handle the babies a lot after they are born. By the time you get your pets, they should

An animal shelter can be a good place to look for a pet rat.

be gentle and tame. Breeders can give you information on the rats' background. They can also answer any questions you might have.

An animal rescue shelter is another good place to look for pet rats. People often think shelters have only dogs and cats. But there are many pet rats in rescue shelters that need homes, too.

A pet store may seem like an obvious place to get a pet rat, but it's not really the *best* choice. Workers often don't know a lot about the animals. They don't take care of the pets the way a breeder would. Many pet store rats have health problems. They may not be as sweet and gentle as those raised by a breeder, either. Many pet store rats are "feeder rats." These rats are sold as snacks for big snakes, such as boas and pythons.

How Many Rats Should You Get?

Rats are social creatures by nature. In the wild, they live in large family groups. So as pets, rats need company. If you have only one pet rat, it will get lonely. No matter how much time you spend with it, it also needs to be with other rats. So you should keep at least two pet rats.

Don't worry that having more than one rat will make them less friendly. Rats kept in groups are still people-friendly, as long as they are handled often.

Rats like to have company, so it's best to have at least two.

Male or Female?

Both males and females make good pets. Males are larger and heavier than females. They are also lazier. They are normally perfectly happy sitting on your lap or being cradled in your arms. Females, on the other hand, are much more playful and full of energy. They love running around and checking things out. They are really curious about things around them. It is often hard to get them to sit and snuggle with you. Some females may calm down as they get older and become lap rats.

It is not a good idea to keep male and female rats together. Otherwise, you will end up with *a lot* of rat babies. However, a vet can do surgery on

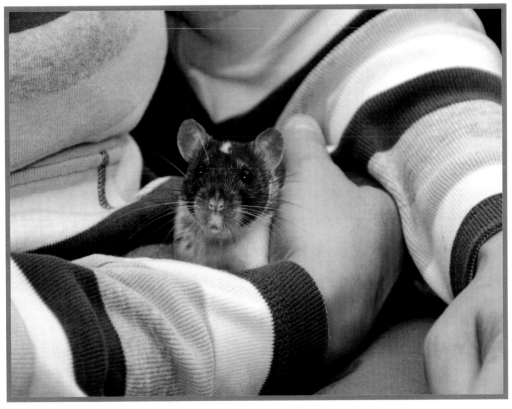

A tame rat may sit in your lap like a dog or cat would.

your rats so they can't make babies. Then you can keep one of each.

Some rats may get territorial, like they are in the wild. (Territory is the place where an animal lives, eats, and sleeps.) They may fight over territory.

Far Out!

Oh, Baby!

A female rat can start having babies as early as five weeks of age. She'll probably have eight to twelve babies at a time. She could even have as many as twenty! In another five weeks or so, her babies will be able to breed, too. If you let your rats continue to breed, you will have dozens of rats in a short time. Soon you'll have more rats than you know what to do with!

For pet rats, the territory is the cage. The rats may mark their territory with their pee. Pet rats may sprinkle drops of pee in different spots around the cage. This acts as a warning to trespassing rats. If you let your pets roam outside their cage, they may also pee on various spots around the room. Some may even mark their owners!

Your rats will get along better if you get them all around the same time. The best age to get them is about six to ten weeks old. Then they will all grow up together as part of the same group.

3

Caring for Your Rats

A rat is not the kind of pet you want running loose when nobody's home. You never know what kind of trouble it might get into. It can sneak under furniture, hide in closets, or crawl behind the walls! Your rat may get lost, escape outside, or get hurt.

A rat on the loose can cause a lot of damage to things in your house. So when you're not playing with your pet rats, you should keep them in a cage. That's the best way to keep them safe when no one is watching them.

Rat-Proof Your Home

Before you bring home your rats, you need to "rat-proof" your house. Make sure your pets can't get into anything they're not supposed to. Your rats will want to look around and check things out.

To keep your rat from getting lost or hurt, you should always keep it in a cage when you're not playing with it.

Some people let their pet rats out of the cage to roam around for an hour or two each day. If you do, it's important not to let them out of your sight. It would be better to keep them in a "playpen" with plenty of toys. A kiddie wading pool makes a

It's nice to let your rat roam around the house for a little while as long as you keep an eye on it.

good playpen for rats. Their toys could be almost anything, from cat or ferret toys to cardboard boxes and tubes.

If you decide to let your rats roam, it is a good idea to pick one room where they can play. That way, it will be easier to keep an eye on them. You may want to throw a blanket or an old sheet over the carpet or furniture. Rats don't care where they poop. Also, remember that rats may mark their territory with drops of pee.

Rats will chew on books, clothes, pencils, papers, and anything else that is around. Keep these things safely put away. Try to put any phone and electrical cords out of your pet's reach.

Are the windows and doors closed? Make sure there is no way your rat can escape. Check the walls, baseboards, and floorboards to make sure there are no cracks or openings. Rats can squeeze through tiny holes—as small as an inch (2.5 cm) wide.

Far Out!

My, What Big Teeth You Have!

Rats love to chew. Like all rodents, it's what they do. In fact, *rodent* comes from a Latin word that means "to gnaw" (bite or chew). Rodents have to chew a lot to keep their teeth short. Their four front teeth—the two on top and two on the bottom—will grow about 4 to 5 inches (10 to 13 cm) in one year! A rat's teeth will continue to grow throughout its entire life.

All the Comforts of Home

What kind of home do pet rats need? Some people keep their rats in a glass tank with a wire-mesh lid. But there are some problems with this type of home. For one thing, fresh air does not flow freely in a tank. So it may become too warm and stuffy. The tank can also get smelly rather quickly. It has to be cleaned often. And you would need a very large and heavy tank to give your rats enough room to run around and explore.

A large wire cage is another choice. The cage should be made of a hard metal. That way the rats won't be able to chew through it. The bottom of the cage should have a solid floor. A wire floor can hurt their tiny feet. Cover the flooring with aspen shavings or paper bedding. Do not use cedar or pine shavings. These materials are poisonous and can make the rats very sick. Wire cages have to be cleaned often. The rats may also make a mess outside the cage by poking bits of food and bedding out through the wire mesh.

A metal cage is a good choice because your rats can't chew through it. Make sure your rats have toys and a place to sleep!

The cage should be big enough for the rats to move around—the bigger the better. Rats love to climb. Wire cages usually have at least two levels. If there is enough room, you can add ramps, shelves, ladders, and ropes. There should a hammock for resting.

Your rats also need soft places to sleep and hide. You can use a small box with bedding. If you give them paper (without ink), tissues, or paper towels, they will make a comfortable nest. With their sharp teeth, they will shred these items into fine bits and place them in the sleeping area. Fresh hay also makes good bedding.

The cage should have a bowl for food. It should be heavy enough so it won't tip over. Rats also need water available at all times. You can use a pet water bottle that hooks onto the outside of the cage. Then they can take sips of water when they are thirsty.

Rats usually "do their business" in the same place—often a corner of the cage. Once you figure

You should provide your rat with a place to make a bed. Fresh hay is a nice bed for a rat.

out exactly where that is, you can put a small litter box (lined with shavings or pellets) in that spot. Then you can scoop it out when it gets too dirty. The whole cage should be cleaned out at least once a week. Shavings and bedding should be replaced.

Are Pet Rats Dirty?

Pet rats are *not* dirty animals. They actually like to be clean. In fact, they bathe themselves often. They lick themselves clean, much like cats do.

Rats like to play, so make sure your rats have lots of toys.

Rats get bored easily. Make sure your pets have lots of toys. These toys can be cardboard boxes, rope toys, and cardboard tubes or plastic pipes for tunnels. Toys for ferrets or parrots are good, too. Blocks of wood, rawhide chew sticks, and cooked soup bones are good for chewing. A rat-sized wheel is good for exercise. Toys that exercise the rats' brains are good, too—for example, puzzle boxes that a rat can open to get a food treat.

Food for Thought

What do you feed rats? Most people buy whatever rat food they find in a pet store. This is usually a loose grain mix. Even though it's mostly healthy, rats don't always eat the healthy stuff. They tend to pick and choose their favorite parts and leave the rest. As a result, they don't get a balanced meal.

Many rat breeders say the main part of the diet should be laboratory pellets. (They are also known as lab blocks or rodent chow.) Lab blocks contain all the important nutrients rats need for a healthy diet. Everything is stuck together in one block. So the rats must chew through the whole thing.

Fresh fruits and vegetables make great treats. And they're healthy, too! Some favorite fruits are apples, cherries, grapes, bananas, strawberries, and melons. Vegetables may include raw broccoli,

It is important for rats to eat
fresh fruits and vegetables.

potatoes, peas, carrots, and cooked sweet potato.
Bits of cooked meat, such as liver and other lean
meats, are also a nice treat once in a while. Rats
also love chicken bones. They aren't bad for the
rats, like they are for dogs. Rats don't swallow the
chicken bones whole—they chew them into bits.

Other foods may include healthy breakfast
cereals, brown rice, whole wheat pasta and bread,
small dog biscuits, and yogurt. Sounds like a lot for

Can't We Get Along?

Can pet rats get along with cats and dogs? Maybe. But you should never leave your rats alone with your other pets. By nature, cats and dogs hunt rats. They are more likely to kill a rat than to want to be its friend. But that doesn't mean it's not possible. You could try to introduce your pets to each other carefully every day. Eventually, they may get used to one another.

such a little rat, doesn't it? Rats don't actually eat huge amounts of food in one sitting. They eat tiny amounts at various times of the day. Just make sure you don't feed your rats too many treats. Then they may not eat their lab blocks. And you may end up with fat rats.

4

Rat Training

Dogs are not the only pets that can learn tricks. Rats are very smart, too. Like any dog, your rat can learn its name. It can also learn a lot of commands many dogs know, including "come," "fetch," and "stay." Some rats can even learn to sit up and beg!

Training a rat takes time, however. Don't expect it to happen overnight. The best thing you can do is to spend time with your pets. When your rats learn to trust you, they will be easier to train.

Your rat can learn to do tricks. This rat is learning to go through a tube on command.

Getting to Know Your Rats

Before you can start rat training, you and your rats need to spend time getting to know each other. Pet rats need at least an hour of play time every day. The more time you spend with them, the friendlier they will become. Spending a lot of time with your pets will make them feel safe and happy.

How Smart Are Rats?

Scientists have done many studies to see just how smart rats really are. What did they find? One study showed that the rats could tell the difference between spoken Dutch and Japanese. That means they actually pay attention to human speech. Several studies showed that rats seem to know how to count and even add! They can also figure out how to get through complicated mazes. They even remember the right way when they run through the same maze again.

Research has also shown that a rat that grows up in a boring, empty cage without toys will have more trouble learning. Play time is very important in helping a rat's brain develop. So is one-on-one time with its owner.

As your rats feels more comfortable, they may enjoy riding on your shoulder while you walk around. You can also let your pets ride in your shirt pocket. They might even give you a lick.

Rats love to play games. That's a good way to get to know your pets. You can let your rats run through cardboard tubes. You can "play catch" with your rats by tossing a little ball back and forth.

Rats are very smart. They can be trained to run mazes.

Purring Like a Rat?

When a dog wags its tail, you know it's happy. A purring cat is letting you know it's happy, too. But what about a rat? A rat will do something called bruxing. It grinds its teeth together. Rats often do this when they are being petted. (It's like a cat's purring.) If a rat is bruxing really hard, its eyes may bug out! This may look weird, but don't worry! It just means that the rat is happy.

You and your rats can play "tug of war" by pulling on the ends of a rope. Like a kitten, a rat will wrestle with your hand or chase a string. You can create a maze for your rats out of blocks. Watch them follow the different paths until they find their reward at the end—a treat!

Trick *and* Treat

The best way to train a rat is to give it treats. Food makes the perfect treat. You may use tiny bits of fresh fruit or vegetables, or something else your rats really like. Whenever your pet does what

you want it to, reward it with a treat. Repeat your commands over and over to help it learn. Give your rats lots of praise, too, when they do something right. Rats love attention. But keep the lessons short so your rats won't get tired or bored.

It is especially important to teach your rats the word "no." This can be helpful when they're chewing something they're not supposed to. Use a

Rats can do gymnastics like rope climbing and jumping through hoops.

firm tone when you scold them and take them away from the forbidden object. Otherwise, you'll find them chewing on the furniture or your favorite sneakers.

Rats are like little gymnasts. They can climb up and down ropes with ease. Their excellent balance makes them natural tightrope walkers. They can even learn to hop through a hoop. You can also teach your rat to fetch a small object and bring it back to you!

It's easy to see why rats make such cool pets. They quickly learn to recognize their owner. They love to snuggle and be petted. Some even give kisses! It doesn't take long to get attached to these cute little critters.

Words to Know

breed—To mate animals and raise their young; *or* a group of animals with similar characteristics, produced by careful choice of the parents.

breeder—A person who breeds animals.

bruxing—Grinding teeth; in rats, may lead to eye popping.

rodent—A small animal with big front teeth used for chewing; rodents include rats, mice, squirrels, and guinea pigs.

territory—The area where an animal lives and gets its food. Some animals will defend their home territory against others of their own kind.

Learn More

Books

Armentrout, David, and Patricia Armentrout. *The Facts on Rats.* Vero Beach, Fla.: Rourke Publishing, 2010.

Fields-Babineau, Miriam. *Rat Training.* Irvine, Calif.: BowTie Press, 2009.

Johnson, Jinny. *Rats and Mice.* Mankato, Minn.: Black Rabbit Books, 2009.

Mancini, Julie R. *Rats.* Neptune City, N.J.: TFH Publications, Inc., 2008.

Web Sites

American Fancy Rat and Mouse Association: Kid's Guide. <http://www.afrma.org/kidsguide.htm>

RATS: Rat Assistance & Teaching Society. <http://www.petrats.org>

Index